GW01086836

Jizzen

By the same author

Jizzen

KATHLEEN JAMIE

PICADOR

First published 1999 by Picador
an imprint of Macmillan Publishers Ltd
25 Eccleston Place, London SW1W 9NF
Basingstoke and Oxford
Associated companies throughout the world
www.macmillan.co.uk

ISBN 0 330 36915 6

3 5 7 9 8 6 4 2

A CIP catalogue record for this book is available from
the British Library.

Printed and bound in Great Britain by
Mackays of Chatham plc, Chatham, Kent

For Phil Butler
love-poet, carpenter

and Duncan, and Freya

I would like to acknowledge the editors of the following publications, where some of these poems first appeared:

Penguin Modern Poets, *The Bloomsbury Anthology of New Scottish Writing*, *Times Literary Supplement*, the *London Review of Books*, *The New Statesman & Society*, *Poetry Review*, *Landfall* (New Zealand), *Columbia* (USA).

The sequence 'Ultrasound' is part of a longer work commissioned by BBC Radio 4.

'Lucky Bag' was commissioned by the National Museum of Scotland.

The short quotation beneath the dedication is from Michael Longley's poem 'Tree-House'.

Grateful thanks are also due to the Scottish Arts Council, and the Paul Hamlyn Foundation.

Contents

.

Crossing the Loch

Remember how we rowed toward the cottage
on the sickle-shaped bay,
that one night after the pub
loosed us through its swinging doors
and we pushed across the shingle
till water lipped the sides
as though the loch mouthed 'boat'?

I forget who rowed. Our jokes hushed.
The oars' splash, creak, and the spill
of the loch reached long into the night.
Out in the race I was scared:
the cold shawl of breeze,
and hunched hills; what the water held
of deadheads, ticking nuclear hulls.

Who rowed, and who kept their peace?
Who hauled salt-air and stars
deep into their lungs, were not reassured;
and who first noticed the loch's
phosphorescence, so, like a twittering nest
washed from the rushes, an astonished
small boat of saints, we watched water shine
on our fingers and oars,
the magic dart of our bow wave?

It was surely foolhardy, such a broad loch, a tide,
but we live – and even have children
to women and men we had yet to meet
that night we set out, calling our own
the sky and salt-water, wounded hills

dark-starred by blaeberries, the glimmering anklets
we wore in the shallows
as we shipped oars and jumped,
to draw the boat safe, high at the cottage shore.

The Graduates

If I chose children they'd know
stories of the old country, the place
we never left. I swear

I remember no ship
slipping from the dock,
no cluster of hurt, proud family

waving till they were wee
as china milkmaids
on a mantelpiece,

but we have surely gone,
and must knock
with brass kilted pipers

the doors to the old land;
we emigrants of no farewell
who keep our bit language

in jokes and quotes;
our working knowledge
of coal-pits, fevers, lost

like the silver bangle I lost
at the shows one Saturday,
tried to conceal, denied

but they're not daft.
And my bright, monoglot bairns
will discover, misplaced

3

among the bookshelves,
proof, rolled in a red tube:
my degrees, a furled sail, my visa.

Forget It

History in a new scheme. I stretch
through hip, ribs, oxter, bursting
the cuff of my school shirt, because
this, Mr Hanning, is me.
'Sir! Sir! Sir!
– he turns, and I claim
just one of these stories,
razed places, important as castles,
as my own. *Mum!*

We done the slums today!
I bawled from the glass
front door she'd long desired.
What for? bangs the oven shut,
Some history's better forgot.
        So how come
we remember the years
before we were born? Gutters
still pocked with fifties rain,
trams cruised dim
street-lit afternoons; war
at our backs. The black door
of the close wheezed
till you turned the third stair
then resounded like cannon.
A tower of bannisters. Nana
and me toiled past windows
smeared in blackout, condemned
empty stone. The neighbours had flitted
to council-schemes, or disappeared . . .

Who were the disappeared? Whose
the cut-throat
razor on the mantelpiece, what man's
coat hung thick with town gas, coal
in the lobby press?
                    And I mind
being stood, washed like a dog
with kettle and one cold tap
in a sink plumbed sheer
from the window
to the back midden
as multistoreys rose
across the goods yard,
and shunters clanked
through nights shared
in the kitchen recess bed.

*I dreamed about my sister in America
I doot she's dead.* What rural
feyness this? Another sibling
lost in Atlantic cloud,
a hint of sea in the rain –
the married in England,
the drunken and the mad,
a couple of notes postmarked Canada,
then mist: but this is a past
not yet done, else how come
our parents slam shut, deny
like criminals: *I can't remember, cannae
mind*, then turn at bay: *Why?*

Who wants to know? Stories
spoken through the mouths

of closes: who cares
who trudged those worn stairs,
or played in now rubbled back greens?
*What happened about my granddad? Why
did Agnes go? How come
you don't know*

that stories are balm,
ease their own pain, contain
a beginning, a middle –
and ours is a long driech
now-demolished street. *Forget it!*
Forget them that vanished,
voted with their feet,
away for good
or ill through the black door
even before the great clearance came,
turning tenements outside-in,
exposing gas pipes, hearths
in damaged gables, wallpaper
hanging limp and stained
in the shaming rain.

History, Mr Hanning.
The garden shrank for winter,
and mum stirred our spaghetti hoops
not long before she started back
part-time at Debenhams
to save for Christmas,
the odd wee
luxury, our first
foreign
holiday.

The Garden of Adam and Dot

The garden blooms under the eye
of the terrible Dot.
She casts out all beasts, while Adam
snaps shut the wicket gate
and his black case,
awa tae the Masons
with just a daft pinny
to cover his shame.

The Barrel Annunciation

I blame the pail
set under our blocked kitchen rhone
which I slopped across the yard

and hoisted to the butt's
oaken rim seven
or nine times in that spring storm;

so plunging rain upon the rain
held in its deep hooped belly
and triggering, unwittingly

without a counter-act of spillage,
some arcane craft laid
like a tripwire or snare,

lore, which, if I'd known,
would have dismissed as dupery
– a crone's trick,

sold to the barren at her cottage door
for a dull coin
or a skirt-length of homespun.

The Bogey-wife

She hoists her thigh over back fences,
her feet squash
worms, hands stained brown as dung.

She flusters hens, looking for babies:
one eye swivelling in the middle of her forehead,
leaves, like the yeti,
the proof of her footprint.

She's simple, gets tangled in the netting
of raspberry groves; but canny – keeps
to the railway wall, the kitchen-midden.

She can *smell* babies, will push
between laundry hung to dry
arms, strong as plum-boughs
twisting into fruit,

and the old wives run her out of town,
some banging pot-lids as others shout
This is private property! Ye've nae right!

But she is charming when cornered,
speaks a nice Scots,
wears a fresh T-shirt
and attractive batik trousers.

Ultrasound

(for Duncan)

i. Ultrasound

Oh whistle and I'll come to ye,
my lad, my wee shilpit ghost
summonsed from tomorrow.

Second sight,
a seer's mothy flicker,
an inner sprite:

this is what I see
with eyes closed;
a keek-aboot among secrets.

If Pandora
could have scanned
her dark box,

and kept it locked –
this ghoul's skull, punched eyes
is tiny Hope's,

hauled silver-quick
in a net of sound,
then, for pity's sake, lowered.

ii. Solstice

To whom do I talk, an unborn thou,
sleeping in a bone creel.

Look what awaits you:
stars, milk-bottles, frost
on a broken outhouse roof.

Let's close the door,
and rearrange
the dark red curtain.

Can you tell the days are opening,
admit a touch more light,
just a touch more?

iii. Thaw

When we brought you home in a taxi
through the steel-grey thaw
after the coldest week in memory
– even the river sealed itself –
it was I, hardly breathing,
who came through the passage to our yard
welcoming our simplest things:
a chopping block, the frost-
split lintels; and though it meant a journey
through darkening snow,
arms laden with you in a blanket,
I had to walk to the top of the garden,
to touch, in a complicit
homage of equals, the spiral
trunks of our plum trees, the moss,
the robin's roost in the holly.
Leaning back on the railway wall,
I tried to remember;
but even my footprints were being erased
and the rising stars of Orion
denied what I knew: that as we were
hurled on a trolley through swing doors to theatre
they'd been there, aligned on the ceiling,
        ablaze with concern
for that difficult giving,
before we were two, from my one.

iv. February

To the heap of nappies
carried from the automatic
in a red plastic basket

to the hanging out, my mouth
crowded with pegs;
to the notched prop

hoisting the wash,
a rare flight of swans,
hills still courying snow;

to spring's hint sailing
the westerly, snowdrops
sheltered by rowans –

to the day of St Bride, the first
sweet-wild weeks of your life
I willingly surrender.

v. Bairnsang

Wee toshie man,
        gean tree and rowan
gif ye could staun
yer feet wad lichtsome tread
granite an saun,
but ye cannae yet staun
sae maun courie tae ma airm
an greetna, girna, Gretna Green

Peedie wee lad
        saumon, siller haddie
gin ye could rin
ye'd rin richt easy-strang
ower causey an carse,
but ye cannae yet rin
sae maun jist courie in
and fashna, fashna, Macrahanish Sand

Bonny wee boy
        peeswheep an whaup
gin ye could sing, yer sang
wad be caller
as a lauchin mountain burn
but ye cannae yet sing
sae maun courie tae ma hert
an grieve nat at aa, Ainster an Crail

My ain tottie bairn
          sternie an lift
gin ye could daunce, yer daunce
wad be that o life itsel,
but ye cannae yet daunce
sae maun courie in my erms
and sleep, saftly sleep, Unst and Yell

vi. Sea Urchin

Between my breast
and cupped hand,
       your head

rests as tenderly
as once I may
       have freighted

water, or drawn
treasure, whole
      from a rockpool

with no premonition
of when next I find one
cast up
      broken.

vii. Prayer

Our baby's heart, on the sixteen-week scan
was a fluttering bird, held in cupped hands.

I thought of St Kevin, hands opened in prayer
and a bird of the hedgerow nesting there,

and how he'd borne it, until the young had flown
– and I prayed: this new heart must outlive my own.

The Tay Moses

What can I fashion
for you but a woven
creel of river-
rashes, a golden
oriole's nest, my gift
wrought from the Firth –

and choose my tide: either
the flow, when, watertight
you'll drift to the uplands –
my favourite hills; held safe
in eddies, where salmon, wisdom
and guts withered in spawn,
rest between moves – that
slither of body as you were born –

or the ebb, when the water
will birl you to snag
on reeds, the river-
pilot leaning over the side:
'Name o God!' and you'll change hands:
tractor-man, grieve, farm-wife
who takes you into her
competent arms

even as I drive, slamming
the car's gears,
spitting gravel on tracks
down between berry-fields,
engine still racing, the door wide
as I run toward her, crying
LEAVE HIM! Please,
it's okay, he's mine.

A Miracle

When the lassie who started it
insisted on TV that she
and her wee brother

had seen the statue of John Knox
shoogle on its pedestal, and milk
tears start in his stony eyes,

from behind the bings, the buses arrived.
Tribes of auld wimmin
and their simpleton sons

filed through the yetts
settled under rugs
and rustled their sweeties.

Gobs of tallow stuck to the plinth.
Babies' booties dangled
from that upflung arm.

So began the custom
whereby, on a certain Sunday,
Knox, adorned in tinsel

gets carted on a bier
round the Edinburgh wynds;
pipers lead the way,

playing 'Comin' Through the Rye'.
By then the lass had disappeared.
– Until, that is, years later,

when, a famously glamorous
Hollywood actress, she announced
her intention to retire

home to Scotland,
buy Holyrood Palace,
and stand for president.

Bonaly

How did we discover our neat fit?
That critical inch, letting her slip
beneath my right arm, her left
snug on my waist? She had the practised
step of a sword-dance medallist,
and I was sensible, possessed
a Girl Guide uniform
stamped and stamped with badges;

and knew how tight to tie
the maroon cotton strip. Ach
it would all go to hell soon enough,
but just that once, on a school pitch
in a Wimpey scheme in Midlothian,
me and Fiona Murray
could beat all comers, pounding
past our shrieking classmates

with our two heads, three legs
like some abomination
the midwife might have smothered
and for what? All for the greater
glory of Bonaly, our House, denoted
by a red sash and named for a loch
somewhere high in the Pentlands –
a place we could scarcely imagine. *Bonaly!*

Mrs McKellar, her martyrdom

Each night she fills, from the fabled
well of disappointment, a kettle
for her hottie. Lying
in his apportioned bed:
Mr McKellar – annulled
beside his trouser press.

Who mentions, who defers to whom
on matters concerning
redecorating the living room,
milk delivery, the damp
stain spreading on the ceiling

when a word is a kind of touch?
Speaking of which, and they don't,
the garden needs attention
and the bedroom window frames,
exquisitely, the darkening hills,
a sky teased with mauve.

But he won't notice, or smell her burning
fix it! fix it!
won't look up the number
of Roofer and Son about that
slightly bewildering stain,

and she'll keep schtum.
Medieval in a dressing gown,
she'd rather display
toward an indifferent world
the means of her agony:
a broken toilet seat,

or die, lips sealed, regarding
the rotting window sills, that
wobbling shelf, which she could
as it happens, repair herself,
but won't, on principle.

Flower-sellers, Budapest

In the gardens
of their mild southern crofts, their
end-of-the-line hillside vineyards,
where figs turn blue, and peppers dry
strung from the eaves,
old women move among flowers,
each with a worn knife, a sliver
crooked in the first finger
of her right hand –
each, like her neighbours,
drawing the blade
onto the callus of her thumb,
so flowers, creamy dahlias,
fall into their arms; the stems'
spittle wiped on their pinafores.

Then, when they have enough,
the old women
foregather at the station
to await the slow, busy little train
that will take them to the city,
where families drift between mass
and lunch; and they hunker
at bus depots, termini
scented with chrysanthemums,
to pull from plastic buckets
yellows, spicy russets,
the petally nub of each flower
tight as a bee;
and from their pockets, pink ribbon
strictly for the flowers.

We must buy some,
– though they will soon wither –
from this thin-faced
widow in a headscarf, this mother
perhaps, of married daughters
down at the border –
or *this* old woman, sat
among pigeons and lottery kiosks,
who reaches towards us to proffer
the morning's fresh blooms;
or the woman there who calls 'Flowers!'
in several languages –
one for each invasion:

We must buy some,
because only when the flowers are dispersed
will the old women head for home,
each with her neighbours,
back where they came, with their
empty buckets and thick aprons
on a late morning train.

The Courtyard

Within the darkwood
yetts, a wrought-
iron gate.

Between myself and her:
arrangements of geraniums,
a conduit's
cool, blue, irrigating vein.

It's always as though
she has just gone
– suggestions of oils,
fruit, a lace fan
on shaded walls,
always as though
a moment ago.

Water trickles.
A blackbird flicks its tail
beside the courtyard's well.

The Black and White Minstrel Show

Out there lay the dark continent, hot
with our mums and dads
and the Heidie. We were fevered
with nerves, suddenly *on*,
doing what we'd practised all term . . .

What did we know
of Al Jolson? What did we know
of the South, here in Midlothian?
We had one Gaelic-speaking boy,
and briefly, an Australian;

we just waved our sweet hands
under the stage lights: *The sun
shines east, the sun shines west,*
. . . my heart strings tangled around
a wee harled school in the rain

where we were 'the lassies',
stood in a row in our starched dirndl
party-frocks, giving it '*doo-dah!*'
And, perhaps, beginning to wonder
how only boys got to fall on one knee

at the last bar of 'Mammy'
– how only boys got to be Black.
But we crossed our neat ankles
and bobbed, suspicious
the high streamers of whistles

were really for them, the laddies,
who milked it, waving and bowing
as the curtain came down on their
boot-polished faces, their grins,
the astonishing whites of their eyes.

Song of Sunday

A driech day, and nothing to do
bar watch starlings fluchter
over soup bones
left on a plate on the grass.
All forenoon broth-barley, marrowfat peas
swelled in a kitchen jug,
and I soaked stamps, corners
torn from polite white envelopes
in a saucer till they peeled clear,
neither soggy nor still stuck: 'See,
watch and not tear them, wait at peace.'

> There'd aye be women
> in the kitchen, brisket
> lashed in string, tatties
> peeled lovelessly, blinded
> pale and drowned. *See if one*
> *now nicked herself*
> *with a paring knife*
> *and spellbound, the house froze –*
> *only now, hacking back in*
> *through privet and rowan,*
> *toward my father caught*
> *mid stretch and yawn,*
> *my wee sister playing Sindys*
> *with the girl next door,*
> *could I wake them*
> *with something alien*
> *and lovely*
> *as a kiss.*

– and we'd be called to eat
what's put in front of us: potatoes, meat
till we could get down, *Please*.
There were African leopards on TV
and *Songs of Praise*. My stamps were dry,
the odd USA, Magyar Poste exotic
among the tuppenny-ha'penny pinks,
the wee lion
rampant in a corner
and after homework I'd have time
to turn to 'Great Britain'
like I'd been shown,
fold and align the edges
with the orderly squares.
Press. 'Bedtime!' *There*.

Hackit

(after a photograph in the museum of Sault Ste-Marie, Ontario)

For every acre cleared, a cairn's raised:
a woman, staggering, stone
after stone in her hands. Desire's

wiped from her eyes,
who once touched to her face
all the linen a bride might need,

her sister closing
till their hands met, sheets
folded and stowed in the hold,

and the gatherings of land –
Arran, Bute, the Heads of Ayr
parted as the ship sailed.

Snow layers fields, and trees blur.
She stares from a door,
fingers splayed, face

hackit
under the lace mutch
brought from her box.

But they'd still recognize
her accent, when steadily
she told about surviving

their first winter:
the flour barrels, empty,
the last herring, small as her hand.

Pioneers

It's not long ago. There were,
after all, cameras
to show us these wagons and blurred dogs,
this pox of burnt stump-holes
in a clearing. Pioneers;
their remains now strewn
across the small-town
museums of Ontario:
the axe and plough, the grindstone,
the wife by the cabin door
dead, and another sent for.

Suitcases

Piled high in a corner of a second-hand store
in Toronto: of course,
it's an immigrant country. Sometimes

all you can take is what you can carry
when you run: a photo, some clothes,
and the useless dead-weight

of your mother tongue.
One was repaired
with electrician's tape – a trade

was all a man needed. A girl,
well, a girl could get married. Indeed
each case opened like an invitation:

the shell-pink lining, the knicker-
like pockets you hook back
with a finger to look

for the little linked keys.
I remember how each held a wraith
of stale air, and how the assistant seemed

taken aback by my accent;
by then, though, I was headed for home,
bored, and already pregnant.

Lochan

(For Jean Johnstone)

When all this is over I mean
to travel north, by the high

drove roads and cart tracks
probably in June,

with the gentle dog-roses
flourishing beside me. I mean

to find among the thousands
scattered in that land

a certain quiet lochan,
where water lilies rise

like small fat moons,
and tied among the reeds,

underneath a rowan,
a white boat waits.

Rhododendrons

They were brought under sail
from a red-tinged east,
carried down gangplanks
in dockers' arms. Innocent
and rare. Their thick leaves
bore a salt-damp gleam,
their blooms a hidden gargle
in their green throats.

Shuddering on trains
to Poolewe, or Arduine,
where the head gardener leaned
across the factor's desk. On a hill
above the sparkling loch
he spoke to his hands,
and terraces were cut,
sites marked, shallow holes dug

before they were turned out.
– Such terribly gentle
work, the grasping of the fat
glazed pots, the fertile
globe of the root-ball
undisturbed, Yunnan
or Himalayan earth
settled with them.

So we step out from their shade
to overlook Loch Melfort
and the bare glens, ready now
to claim this flowering, purple
flame-bright exotica as our own;
a commonplace, native
as language or living memory,
to our slightly acid soil.

Whirligig

On a croft with two trees
at the top of the glen,
a chimney cowl birls,

its glances of sunlight
transmit to the mirror
of an idling post office van,

to be flashed to a house with a black
and white collie, the washing
in code on the – ahem – *carousel*.

Interregnum

So I'm moving between rooms
with a tray, advertising
McEwan's, the kind we took sledging
those distant snow-bright afternoons

– or funereal lacquer, with peonies,
or that classic of my mother's:
a view of Windsor Castle
inside a wicker pale. Whatever

– a tray, and on it:
two glasses of Vouvray. Or better:
croissants and cafetière, my lover
outstretched on the duvet,

or – dream on – pizza for one
and *Prime Suspect*.
No matter. I'm at the door now
casting round wildly

trying to find someplace
to set the thing down,
looking round madly,
and I realize exactly

how I'll end up:
one legged, unbalanced,
trying to hold steady
this jigsaw, this haggis

this model-to-scale
of the SS *Balmoral*,
while howking toward me
the so-called 'occasional' table,

and swiping it clear
of *Spot on the Farm*
for the sake of this precious
whatever-I've-brought

from the place I've just left,
– a clear space
I can't very well
turn round and reclaim,

because it won't now exist.
Besides, that's a trifle
defeatist. Besides,
what's the point of a tray?

Lucky Bag

Tattie scones, St Andra's banes,
a rod-and-crescent Pictish stane,
a field o whaups, organic neeps,
a poke o Brattisani's chips;
a clootie well, computer bits,
an elder o the wee free Kirk;

a golach fi Knoydart,
a shalwar-kemeez;
Dr Simpson's anaesthetics, *zzzzzzzz*,
a gloup, a clachan, a Broxburn bing,
a giro, a demo, Samye Ling;

a ro-ro in the gloaming,
a new-born Kirkcaldy
baby-gro; a Free State, a midden,
a chambered cairn –
yer Scottish lucky-bag, one for each wean;
please form an orderly   rabble.

The Soldier

They're still clan here, Wilkies and Melvilles;
names painted on plumbers' and joiners' vans
are those carved out, regiment by regiment
under the soldier in his stone kilt.

He still holds his rifle, almost gently,
as you'd touch the uncertain
neck of a dog, his beret still tilted,
pockets stuffed with baccy, letters from home.

Below him, though he'd never know,
four benches face the plinth; but the mothers
favour the play-park sloping under trees
toward the river, with trampolines and swings.

– Benches, and borders laid only last week
by a squad of council gardeners:
two men, a gaffer, and a daft-looking laddie
who pulled up with marigolds trembling in a trailer

while the soldier kept watch. Traffic passed,
Ford Fiestas, bass-beat pounding,
and a tractor, too far to be heard,
turned up and down, baling hay or something,

while below, behind his angle of land,
this summer afternoon, late in the century:
just the old folks' lovely thunk of bowls
a call, applause, a small sufficiency.

The Well at the Broch of Gurness

Imagine the sails flying like swans,
women hauling infants
as ox-horns bawled,
and door-bars thudding
home in this socket, where a thrush nests.

And slipping away from the rest
– a girl, crossing flagstones
to the sunken well, where, left hand
on the roof's cool rock,
she steps down out of the world.

Perhaps she's there yet, waiting
till they've done their worst
before she drinks, then barefoot
begins her return toward daylight,
where she'll vanish.

The broch's rubble.
Her homestead's lintels tilt
through mown turf.
But we can follow her, descend
below the bright grasses, the beat of surf

step by hewn step, crouching
till our eyes adjust – before we seek
the same replenishing water,
invisible till reached for,
when reached for, touched.

St Bride's

(For Freya)

So this is women's work: folding
and unfolding, be it linen or a selkie-
skin tucked behind a rock. Consider

the hare in jizzen: her leverets' ears
flat as the mizzen of a ship
entering a bottle. A thread's trick;

adders uncoil into spring. Feathers
of sunlight, glanced from a butterknife
quiver on the ceiling,

and a last sharp twist for the shoulders
delivers my daughter, the placenta
following, like a fist of purple kelp.

The Green Woman

Until we're restored to ourselves
by weaning, the skin jade
only where it's hidden
under jewellery, the areolae still tinged,
– there's a word for women like us.

It's suggestive of the lush
ditch, or even an ordeal,
– as though we'd risen,
tied to a ducking-stool,
gasping, weed-smeared, proven.

Bolus

So little of the world is bequeathed
through us, our gifts
instead, are passed among the living
– like words, or the bolus
of chewed bread
a woman presses with her tongue
into the gorgeous open mouth of her infant.

On the Design Chosen for the New Scottish Parliament Building by Architect Enric Miralles

An upturned boat
  – a watershed.

Meadowsweet

Tradition suggests that certain of the Gaelic
women poets were buried face down.

So they buried her, and turned home,
a drab psalm
hanging about them like haar,

not knowing the liquid
trickling from her lips
would seek its way down,

and that caught in her slowly
unravelling plait of grey hair
were summer seeds:

meadowsweet, bastard balm,
tokens of honesty, already
beginning their crawl

toward light, so showing her,
when the time came,
how to dig herself out –

to surface and greet them,
mouth young, and full again
of dirt, and spit, and poetry.